Boy Drinkers

Other books by Terence Winch

That Special Place: New World Irish Stories (nonfiction), Hanging Loose, 2004

The Drift of Things (poems), The Figures, 2001

The Great Indoors (poems), Story Line Press, 1995

Contenders (stories/fiction), Story Line Press, 1989

Irish Musicians/American Friends (poems), Coffee House Press, 1986

(See www.terencewinch.com)

Boy Drinkers

Terence Winch

Hanging Loose Press
Brooklyn, New York

Published by Hanging Loose Press, 231 Wyckoff Street, Brooklyn, New York, 11217-2208. All rights reserved. No part of this book may be reproduced without the publisher's written permission, except for brief quotations in reviews.

www.hangingloosepress.com

Printed in the United States of America
10 9 8 7 6 5 4 3 2 1

Hanging Loose Press thanks the Literature Program of the New York State Council on the Arts for a grant in support of the publication of this book.

Book cover design by Susan F. Campbell

Acknowledgments:
"Faith Healing," *Smartish Pace*; "Celebration" & "Beach," *Innisfree*; "Human," *Hanging Loose*; "Disgrace" and "Revolution," *Shiny*; "Comfort," "Defiance," and "Boy Drinkers," *The World*; "Audacity" and "Custodian," *Solo*. "Faith," *Donkey Jaw*; "Spell," *The Blue Canary*; "Prayer to St. Patrick," *Irish Music* magazine; "Jesus" first appeared in *ZZZZ*.

"Promises" and "Custodian" first appeared in *New Perspectives on the Irish Diaspora* (Southern Illinois University Press, ed. Charles Fanning).
"Night Shift" first appeared in the chapbook *Total Strangers* (Toothpaste Press).
The poems in "Nuns" were published as a chapbook by that name (Wyrd Press, Janey Tannenbaum, ed.).

"Sinning," words and music, © T. Winch (Celtic Thunder Music/BMI)
The author wishes to thank the Maryland State Arts Commission for its support. Also, special thanks to Dominick Murray, the late Jim Keenan, Jesse Winch, Doug Lang, Will Farrell, Linda Hickman, Patrick J. Clancy, Allison Hazen, and Susan Campbell.

Library of Congress Cataloging-in-Publication Data available on request.

ISBN: 978-1-931236-80-5 (paper)
ISBN: 978-1-931236-81-2 (cloth)

Produced at The Print Center, Inc. 225 Varick St., New York, NY 10014, a non-profit facility for literary and arts-related publications. (212) 206-8465

TABLE OF CONTENTS

I. BOY DRINKERS

II. NUNS

III. O, MARY, I COULD WEEP FOR MIRTH

This book is for Michael Lally

and in memory of John McCarthy

I. Boy Drinkers

COMFORT

Father Ray Byrne quickly became
a star. He played sports, danced,
sang, told jokes. He was a man
of the people, and we loved him
for that. He came to our apartments
and brought us comfort.

He even came to a high school graduation
party one night. I was a little drunk.
Father Byrne came up to me and asked
"Are you thinking about it?" I panicked.
What did he mean? Sex? Booze? Basketball?
Could he read my mind? Then I realized
his tone wasn't accusatory, so I said,
"Yeah, I'm thinking about it," not having
any idea what he was talking about.

"That's great," he said, "I can always
tell when a young man is thinking about
it. Just let me know if I can be of any help."
Now I was positive he wasn't talking about
sex or money or any of the things I actually
did have on my mind. Father Byrne thought
I might have a vocation.

But I wasn't considering the priesthood.
I didn't even think professional basketball
was a possibility any more. God had walked
out the door about a year before,
when I was sixteen, and never looked back,
even though I begged him not
to leave me, alone and weeping
in this valley of tears.

GRACE

We didn't know if he was a retard or a drunk.
He would lurch around Gaelic Park
during game days, grinning like an idiot,
dribbling onto his filthy cassock. First time
I saw him it was a shock. And then his
name, which had a funny sound to it:
Father McMenamin. The drunk priest,
the embarrassment to the whole community.
Happily staggering onto the field, being gently
ushered off again, scolded as one would a
child: now, now, Father, mustn't go there.

The shame of it all. An affliction from God.
The shepherd, the authority, the man of the cloth
as moron, bum, joke. The meaner ones
would buy him drinks and make fun of him.
Give us your blessing, Father. Forgive me
my sins, Father, and I'll give you a glass.
McMenamin forgave them all,
wondering where he was. Somewhere
far from home it seemed, searching
for grace in the darkness of the Bronx.

Angelus

Drowsy in the late morning sun
wet sand stuck to limbs
some of it even in my mouth
the distant sound of swimmers
playing, yelling, splashing
seeming to come from another world
adding to the lull
a radio's mix of song
and static sparking through
the deep heat, as I would lie
there on the blanket
remembering life in the clouds
and caves, the thought-free
animal past encoded in our
bones and almost forgotten

then the bells would begin
the alarm clock from heaven
and all the buzz of life engulfing
me would freeze in place
and everyone would stand
so I had to shake myself
awake and stagger to my feet
and mumble along with the other
talking statues: "the angel
of the Lord declared unto Mary"

I would wonder where
the angels had all gone
why they had all withdrawn:
my guardian angel who
long ago abandoned me
the good angels and bad

the kindergarten angels
in white with wire wings
and all the puerto ricans
named angel

then the prayer ends
the holy visitors go back
to their secret dimension
through a hole in the sky
and life returns to our bodies,
movement makes us fluid again,
and it still only a moment past
noon, still time to fall back
into sleep, waves away from
the other world, at least for now

AUDACITY

Every Catholic in New York cringed
at the sight of him. Holy-Mary
piety, androgynous, nun-like demeanor,
fat cherubic face only made his warlike
politics and egomania seem more intense,
scarier. Inside we all knew he was mean
and vain. Kids from every parish cut down
in Vietnam while Spellman waltzed with
J. Edgar Hoover and built monuments to himself.

Spellman Hall at my college,
other Spellman halls at other schools.
A little archipelago of namesakes.
Even children mocked his audacity.

When Cardinal Spellman High School opened,
in a crummy part of the Bronx in a temporary,
ugly, squat building, no one wanted to go.
But the archdiocese offered incentives
to tempt the flock (an easy ride,
low tuition) and soon enrollment surged.

Even my father, school custodian
and good Catholic, had no use for him.
The Cardinal set up a bogus pension plan
leaving those who had labored a lifetime
for the church with nothing at the end
but a handshake and a shove out the door.
You didn't retire under Spellman.
You worked till you died poor.

CUSTODIAN

for Charlie Fanning

I ran the shovel along the street,
a razor path through the sidewalk face,
snow lather parting for me, for my father,
our feet crunching in the city night.

We grabbed the garbage cans from school
and church and dragged them up the iron
stairs. I lugged burlap bags stuffed
with Bingo cards, light as cream puffs.

We swept the auditorium with green sawdust
from huge drums. We hammered and drilled
in his workshop, where tools hung on pegboard,
their images silhouetted behind them

For instant identification and placement.
Once he sawed his index finger in half
on the power saw in a moment of inattention
in a life otherwise built of skill and care.

Once a year the Monsignor made him climb inside
the giant boiler and clean it out
with enormous pipe cleaners till he was black
with soot that took days to wash off.

Sonny boy, he called me, and laddie buck.
He always said just do your best.
We loved to watch him fall asleep
on the couch, *Daily News* over his face

Snores filling the apartment
with the music of rest well deserved.
His finger took years to heal enough
for him to play the banjo again but a black scar

Ran down its center. He'd give me a rub
with his unshaven face, rough as sandpaper.
He'd pretend he didn't know me, scrubbed from
the tub, the lovely lie delighting me every time.

SPELL

Sometime in 1953 my beautiful sister Eileen
fell under the spell of Bishop Fulton J. Sheen.
His piercing eyes won the hearts of all the Irish girls
and his ratings that year even beat out Milton Berle's.

We watched "Life Is Worth Living" every week
and marveled that so rare a man, who could speak
so miraculously, convert the rich through his amazing powers,
help the poor and squash the Reds, was one of ours.

Mary once sent him a ten-year-old girl in white with a rose
as a sign he shouldn't fret about his fame, expensive clothes,
his dalliances with Clair Booth Luce and Loretta Young.
But then the devil sent him Cardinal Spellman to spoil the fun.

Eileen heard him speak one night that year and was so taken
with him she gave him all she had but for one subway token.

CELEBRATION

In our world, nothing compared
with Midnight Mass on Christmas Eve,
God's power surging through the congregation,
from altar boys in our stiff collars and big red bows
to the solid men of the parish in their finest array:
Blue suits, gold wrist watches, crisp white shirts.
The women perfumed and girdled, lipsticked
and bejeweled. Enough incense
in the air to do the Wise Men proud.

The procession wound through the church,
organ honking, voices lifted in the special
Christmas sense of the slate wiped clean
and the universe beginning anew.
The tree in the house lit with fat colored bulbs
that looked good enough to eat. The old suitcase
full of fragile decorations, buried treasure found
every year on Christmas Eve and set free again.
The baby Jesus alive and well! Herod thwarted!

This called for presents. Toys, games, maybe
a watch or a knife. Along with Jesus came the whole
cast of Yuletide characters—Santa, Rudolph,
the Chipmunks, Bing Crosby, Frosty, Scrooge.
I'm surprised the Easter Bunny didn't crash
the event. My father put out apple pie
and a glass of milk for Sanny, the remaining traces
of which on Christmas morning were proof enough
for me and my brother Jimmy of the entire
supernatural infrastructure of Bronx Irish culture.

But it was the party after Midnight Mass
that I remember most. Relatives and neighbors
would pour into our apartment for an all-nighter.
My mother would get the percolator going,
and start making breakfast for half the parish.
Bacon, eggs, blood pudding, plates of fresh rolls
with poppy seeds bought that day
in the Treat Bakery on Tremont Avenue.

Eating breakfast at two in the morning!
This was a miracle for a ten-year-old boy.
Bottles of Seagram's and Canadian Club
stood at attention on the kitchen table,
silver ice bucket ringed with penguins
awaiting duty beside them. Ladies smoking
and gossiping. Glasses clinking. Laughter
throughout the house. The smell of pine,
the delicious aroma of sizzling bacon,
all welcoming Jesus back for another year.

Then the music and singing would start up,
my father on the banjo, P. J. Conway on the box.
"The Stack of Barley," "The Lakes of Sligo,"
medleys of marches, waltzes, and polkas.
Theresa McNally, from my mother's own town
in Galway, would sing "Galway Bay." Steps would
be danced, jokes told, more drinks mixed and gulped.

I would go to bed so filled with the spirit
it seemed impossible to believe that life could
ever return to normal. Lying there exhausted,
but anxious to sneak down the hall at the earliest
opportunity and tear open the tantalizing packages,
I believed in everything: Jesus our Lord, Santa
our magic benefactor, my parents the immortal source
of the ongoing celebration that could never end.

Boy Drinkers

I had my first drink in a bar
when I was fourteen.
I was big for my age
and had a phony draft card.
Then I drank and drank for years.
We would start
at two or three in the afternoon
and keep on till four a.m.
In the bars in those days
the excitement of intoxication
filled our souls,
made everything pulse,
leaving the material and spiritual
worlds enhanced, illuminated.

When we were sick as children,
my mother gave us blackberry brandy,
and I later developed a taste for it.
When I was in high school,
I would buy a pint of it before going to a dance.
The boy drinkers would assemble
in the boys' bathroom
and guzzle their pints of Scotch
or rye, often polishing off the bottle
in one quick visit. I gulped down
blackberry brandy, the family favorite.

I remember being somewhere in West Farms
in the Bronx, drinking my brandy,
then throwing up over the chain-link fence
in front of Mister Donut.
I liked the sweet sticky
essence of blackberry brandy.

At home, though, we kept a big jug
of Gallo Port right on the floor
in a corner of the kitchen.
My parents enjoyed Gallo Port,
though I never cared for it.

2.
I remember coming home
from school one day, maybe a year earlier,
and finding my mother stretched
sideways across one of the beds
in the room I shared with my brother.
She was crying and I remember
how frightened her weeping made me.
I knew the world would never
be the same again.

My father stayed up with her
every night for years,
after having worked all day.
I learned how to inject my mother
by practicing on oranges.

My father embraces me
and we stand there
in the middle of the living room
holding each other and crying,
as though our huddle could
contain the pain
invading our lives. I hear
my mother say to someone
Thank God Paddy and the boys
are close.

Father Byrne came to visit her,
and this meant a great deal to us.
He was the new handsome priest
who could sing like Bing

and everybody adored him.
When it got really bad, our cause
was taken up by the Dominican Sisters
of the Sick Poor, an order of nuns
each of whom was a registered nurse.
They came every day and demonstrated
what real selflessness looked like.

After she died, we held a benefit
for those nuns and raised
more than a thousand dollars.
Before she died, we moved a TV
into the front room and borrowed
a hospital bed. We all watched
the Nixon-Kennedy debates
in that room, my mother like all
of us amazed an Irishman
might wind up in the White House.

My father never bounced back
and that was hard for me
to accept and made me angry
at him, although I knew his heart
was broken, and every other night
I'd be woken up by his nightmares
and I'd shake him awake
but I already knew at sixteen
how easily we break.

PROMISES

The elevation of our pastor Father Walsh
to monsignor became the parish
dress rehearsal for the Second Coming.
Everyone was mobilized. A big procession
snaked through the neighborhood, with flags
and banners, and virgins scattering flowers
before the litter on which the Monsignor
sat, perched on a throne carried by strong men
of the parish. It was like Caesar entering Rome,
Ike liberating Europe, Lindbergh landing in Paris.

The bishop presided over the ceremony in the church
after which the Monsignor could now dress in a red cape
and wear a biretta with a little red ball on top.
Scared of him before, now we were terrified.

My father was custodian of the parish school,
so the Monsignor was his boss. "What's your name,
little boy?" he asked me on my first day of kindergarten,
as we filed through the school doors. "Don't you know
who I am?" I replied. "My father runs this place."

Sometimes the Monsignor would roam the neighborhood,
his red cape billowing behind him, hunting sinners
as children hid or ran away, and adults crossed the street.

When the Vogue movie house on Tremont Avenue offered
me a job, I went to the rectory and asked the Monsignor
to write me up a bogus baptismal certificate
making me a year older, so I could get the job.
He loved the exercise of power, and in a flash
turned me from fifteen to sixteen.

At age seven, I had gone to him for my first confession.
"Bless me, Father—" I began. "Monsignor," he corrected.
I confessed my misdeeds—forgetting my morning prayers,
talking back to my parents, fighting with my friends.

"Promise me you'll never do these things again," he said.
"I'll try, Father, but I can't promise."
"It's Monsignor," he said.
You don't make promises to God
you know you can't keep,
but I didn't know who
to be more afraid of.
"I'll try, Monsignor."

FORGIVENESS

Father Cahir kept us holy.
He smoked cigars in the confessional.
He had a distracted air about him,
as though he wasn't sure what
he was supposed to do next.

I don't remember what he taught.
History, probably. It was his
liberal attitude as a confessor
that made him a legend.

No matter what you confessed to,
he always barked out the same penance:
"Three Hail Marys and a Good Act
of Contrition. Next!" So we tested
this leniency, confessing
to rape, murder, burglary.

Cahir paid no attention.
He knew we were a bunch
of high school punks.
Puffing his cigar,
he'd issue his standard
penance and absolve all sins,
real or imagined,
with godlike aloofness,
his vast indifference to
or total acceptance of the darkness
within the human soul
exactly how I hope the deity
regards us. Take forgiveness
any way you can get it.

DISGRACE

On Sundays teenage guys would have a few beers
before Mass, then a couple of cigarettes in front
of the church before finally filing in
for the last few minutes of the service,
standing in the back and looking
worse than the suspects in a police lineup.

Hungover and unsure of what
business we even had in this house
of God, we shuffled, coughed, cleared
our throats, laughed, talked, rolled
our eyes, elbowed each other,
checked out the girls,
sacrilege just another joke.
Smirked at the collection
basket. "That's you, pal," we said
to each other if we happened to catch
any of the sermon. Sinners, devils,
atheists. "Got your number, Jack."

Father Hammer glared at us from the pulpit.
Son of a judge, heir to the Hammer soft
drink empire, we were trash to him.
Under Knobby Walsh's thumb for years
till the old Monsignor finally died, Hammer
had the power now, and he would nail us.
No party in the back of his church.

Shuffling and jiving, barely aware
of the drone of his voice, we were struck
suddenly by lightning. Hammer attacked
in fury—"You punks in the back, sit down
and be quiet!" We looked around, stared

up, smiled nervously. Who, us?
"You—McNally, McCarthy, O'Donnell.
That's right. I'm talking to you."

The naming of names. This had never
happened before. The entire congregation
shifted as one, angling their bodies
sideways to witness the great drama unfolding.
All eyes were on us, faces of neighbors,
relatives, friends. "Sit down! C'mon,
that's right, get out of the back.
Scalley, Keenan! I know all of you,
we all do. You're a disgrace,
the lot of you. Sit down."

We started sneaking into the pews,
all of us acting nonchalant.
One or two of our crew ducked out
the front door, the rest of us envying
them their bold escape. I slid into
a seat in the back, my fellow worshippers
inching closer together to make room,
rear ends sliding along the edge of
the pew, everyone eyeing me with disdain.
I shut my eyes, buried my face in my hands
the way we did after Communion,
and floated into the future.

DEFIANCE

Joe Deloria was a scary kid. A mean
little prick, all bad attitude
and in-your-face teenage evil.
Pint-sized, skinny, pocked
with pimples. No one dared tangle
with him. Not the biggest, toughest
kids. Not even the teachers.

Except for Brother Thomas Kelly,
six-foot-five-inch chemistry teacher
from Hell's Kitchen whose hands
were as big as frying pans.
He could palm a basketball
like it was a spaldeen.
He was a nice guy most of the time
but we all knew he had a temper
like a bomb going off in your face.
He commanded absolute respect
from absolutely everybody.

Except Joe Deloria. Deloria hated
everyone and feared no one.
Especially some big Irish fuck
in a cassock and crucifix.
Deloria never talked to any other kids.
You worried about accidentally
bumping into him for fear
he'd go off on you. Not even
Frankie Pearson, who was built
like a boxer and whose cock

was the size of most kids' forearms,
and who died in Vietnam before
the sixties had ended, would
get on the wrong side of Joe Deloria.

One day Brother Kelly, with his
back to the class, was writing
something on the blackboard
when Deloria hissed out "shit"
upon dropping something on the floor.
Kelly stopped writing and all the other
kids froze. Kelly didn't allow
unauthorized talking in his class.
"What did you say, Mr. Deloria?"
he asked. Deloria stared at him.
"Come up here," Brother Kelly
ordered. Deloria slid contemptuously
out of his seat and went
to the front of the room.
David and Goliath. Tiny Deloria
next to towering Kelly.

The rest of us were thrilled
and terrified that this confrontation
was taking place. "What did you
say?" Kelly asked. Deloria looked
up at him with total defiance.
"I asked you a question," Kelly
said, while removing his watch
and rolling up his sleeves.
Fantastic—he was going to kick
Deloria's ass. This would be better
than the professional wrestling
my father watched on TV.

"I'm not going to ask you again,"
Kelly announced. Everyone wondered
what Deloria would do. He was about

eye level with Kelly's cincture.
"Fuck you," Deloria said. His response
was too shocking to cause even
a collective gasp. Complete silence
filled the room. Kelly started
swinging, and Deloria added to his
repertoire of unthinkable acts:
he started swinging back.

Kelly beat him mercilessly,
and Deloria was expelled from
school for good. A week later
he came back with a zip gun,
hunting for Kelly, but never
found him. We heard he threw
the gun onto the subway tracks
just before the cops could get it.

AUTHORITY

Hermano Bernardo taught Spanish.
Chubby, bald, with a five o'clock shadow,
he had no authority. Kids did not
respect him because he never beat us up.
Never even seemed capable of such a thing.
Ineffectual, gentle, kind, he was the perfect
victim. The object of our scorn.

One day in the middle of class,
as Hermano Bernardo taught us
the same fundamentals over and over,
a fly flew into the room and headed right
for the hapless brother. He waved at the fly,
but the insect persisted in tormenting him,
confirming his natural status as target.
We all laughed at his plight. Almost
any other brother would have started
smashing some heads, but Hermano
Bernardo looked flustered and uncertain.

From that day forward, whenever he
entered a room, all of us buzzed like
flies. He pretended not to notice.
His nickname became "The Fly."
No one learned any Spanish.

DISCIPLINE

Father Dardis noticed the letter on my sweater.
I didn't make the junior varsity basketball team,
but I did play in the band and was manager
of the basketball team, running the game clock
and making sure the court was ready for every contest.
So I had earned two letters in sophomore year,
one of which was sewn to my sweater.

"Hey, where'd ya get that letter? You didn't earn
a letter." What is this moron talking about? I thought.
But before I could offer any defense, he grabbed me
by my shirtfront, lifted me off the floor,
and, holding me up against the wall in a deserted
stairway, began to slap me across the face,
first one way, then another. He was six five
and built like a dumptruck. I was a good foot
off the ground during the beating,
and more startled than hurt
by the time he let go and I slid
down the wall
to a complete stop.

He just walked away. All in a day's work.
Kids hated and feared Dardis. He taught
World History and had never had an
original idea in his life. Soon word of our encounter
spread throughout the school. I was sophomore
year president and a good student.
I vowed to seek revenge.

I went to the office of the Dean of Discipline,
Father Fahey. I told him what happened.
Fahey was a quiet, scholarly

man. He was Irish, so was I.
Fahey shook his head as I told
my side of the story. "I'll have
a word with Father Dardis," he said.

Dardis approached me in the gym
a few days later. I tensed up,
not knowing what to expect.
"Sorry about the other day," biting off
each word with a snarl. "I didn't think
you earned that letter." "Well, I did,"
I said, as he marched away, furious
at having to apologize to a kid.
I hate revenge. Its fleeting satisfaction
leaves you feeling bad in the end.

But I loved Fahey after that. I wanted
to hang out with him on the Senior
Walk, smoking cigarettes, discussing
the problem of good and evil.

RETREAT

for Tim Meagher

We were taken somewhere upstate
to meet with God, and I was made
Captain of the Retreat because
I was apparently the first student
in the history of Bishop Dubois High School
to object to the compulsory nature
of this annual ritual that every senior
class from the school's beginnings
in post-war Harlem had to endure.

I had to get up before everyone else,
at 5 a.m., and wander down the long
dark corridors, knocking on doors,
and making sure my peers had arisen.
We couldn't talk, except at certain
designated times. We ate simple
food in the cafeteria. We wandered
the woods and fields around the retreat
house. But mostly we sat in the chapel
and listened to a shifting cast of priests
exhort and rebuke us for hours on end,
in hopes of preserving our Catholicism
beyond graduation in a month.

The priest in charge, a handsome, red-haired
Jesuit named Reilly, stood about six four.
On our last night in what seemed to me
the closest thing to a prison I'd ever
been in, Father Reilly gave a talk on
the Shroud of Turin. We met in the lounge
instead of the chapel, and when we saw that he
was preparing to show color slides, we thought
finally we'd have a bit of entertainment.

A master showman, Reilly took us through
the torture and crucifixion of Jesus
step by step, one gory detail after another,
all verified scientifically by the Shroud slides.

The nails through the wrists, the thorns jammed
into the scalp, the spear stuck into the torso.
The blood everywhere. And the Shroud a photograph
of the entire awful experience, all of which
Christ endured for us lowlifes whose primary
concerns were cigarettes and masturbation.

It was all our fault. We all wanted to confess,
die, and relax in Heaven for eternity.
We wanted to be done with the guilt and confusion.
We would take full responsibility for the murder of Christ.

When I confessed I told Reilly that I felt suicidal.
My mother's death the year before had left me
confused about many things, with sex, of course,
the biggest problem of all. He gave me the name
of a psychologist to see in Queens. I thought, this
will never fly. I was seventeen, it was 1963,
and you were more likely to encounter aliens
singing arias than to so much as hear a word
like "psychologist" in my neighborhood.

My father, who was going through a tough time himself,
became very upset when I told him I might
go see a shrink in Queens. He wanted to know
why I couldn't just tell him instead.
So I dropped the whole idea and
never went to confession again.

Values

I tell people I peaked at seventeen.
Student body president and valedictorian.
Scholarship to college. I practiced my graduation
speech upstairs in a corridor outside the classrooms,
pacing up and down, smoking one smoke after another.
My mother had died the year before, and so
was not in attendance for my triumph.

My father was proud, but still grieving,
which was how he stayed till he died.
I wore a white tuxedo jacket and spoke out
against the failure of moral values, a trend
I later came to exemplify. I had even
published a letter in the *Saturday Review*
in my senior year rebutting an article
that said we were on a downhill skid.
Not here, I wrote back. Not at Bishop
Dubois High School. Here we are pure
and exist only to do good and make
our parents and teachers proud.

But I was just saying what they wanted
to hear. I sat on stage next to Father Harry Hicks,
who had a Ph.D. and taught English lit.
But most surprising of all, he had once been married.
He covered his mouth and made sly, witty jokes
as we sat together on high. I laughed.
I wanted it all to be a joke myself.
I've always been that way. If it's funny,
it hurts less. Success is standing at the podium,
delivering a speech, with everyone thinking

you're great. Failure is the future, the fear
running through you at two in the morning,
a phone ringing somewhere
in the dark house waking you up.

BEACH

A drunk old woman named Aunt Peg
was our landlady. We were seventeen.
We'd come home drunk ourselves, boys
at the beach for a week, and Aunt Peg

Would chase us around the room naked.
It was an ugly sight. We would throw
up in our sleep and wake up in our mess.
Once Aunt Peg tried to get in bed with us.

She had a grown son confined to the basement,
a husband in a bathrobe who never spoke,
her life a B-movie horror story. We were young,
hair thick and dark, muscle definition cutting

Through tight tee-shirts. She was a scary hag.
If the spirit has its own life, let the noises
it makes be as silent as the multiplication
and subtraction of time, and not
the rattle of a cough in the dark.

Now I look at our photos. Old guys, graying,
grizzled, pot-bellied, having a smoke
at the reunion. Wondering
what hit us.

ELEGY

1.
In the photo in my college yearbook
Darby T. Ruane poses with the Supremes.
Red-faced, pot-bellied Brother Ruane,
leading impresario of the Irish Christian
brothers of Iona College. Forget all those vows—
there were stars to schmooze, acts to book,
glamour to stand alongside of. Even in
New Rochelle in the 1960s.

Brother Ruane also taught classes in literature.
He made an odd humming sound when musing
on some particular matter of interest to him:
"Ummmmmm, phenomenology...fascinating!"
An overweight Jack Paar lookalike, full of bluster
and showbiz, he provided great entertainment.
We assumed he thought everything—
college, life, religion, you name it—
was all a scam in the end.
He was one of us.

"Ummm, very good, good point,"
he would say, at any inane student offering.
He would flash his credentials:
"Ummmm, my Ph.D. is in Keats,
the great John Keats. That's the only area
I'm an expert in." He would chuckle.
We would wonder if he remembered
even one line of Keats.
The only thing on his mind was filling
the gym with glitter and basking
in its glorious reflection.
But he had to pretend to care about
Keats, and Shelley, and Byron,
and even Matthew Arnold.

2.
They may have changed it by now,
but if you have the 1962 edition of
Volume 2 of the *Norton Anthology*
of English Literature, you will note
a curious situation on page 898.
On the bottom of that page begins
Arnold's dreary poem "Thyrsis,"
a long elegy for Arthur Hugh Clough.
The title is footnoted number one,
but when you scan down to the note
to find out who this Thyrsis might be,
the words "tuna fish" meet your eye.

You figure out quickly that there are
two footnotes, each with the number one,
the first referring to the word "tunnies" in
"The Scholar Gypsy," which ends on
the same page where "Thyrsis" begins,
and the second number one being
the note on "Thyrsis."

The inevitable, of course, happened.
Zipping through Matthew Arnold and all
his works one day in the sophomore survey
course, Darby was halted by a student
raising his hand to say, "Brother, if Thyrsis
means tuna fish, what is Arnold trying to say?"
Brother Ruane launched into an extended
riff on the significance of tuna fish
in the poem: "Ummmm, it suggests all life
going back to the water, the cyclical nature
of creation, the connectedness of all things."
A brave student finally stopped him:
"Brother, he's looking at the wrong footnote.
Thyrsis doesn't mean tuna fish."

His greatest moment. He never even blinked.
No embarrassment. No awkwardness.
No missing a beat. He had a strategy:
he was sticking to his story.
"True, it doesn't actually mean tuna fish,
but still we must take into account the great
cycle of life, the fish returning to water,
ummmmmm, the great symbols of life and death
revealed in the poem."

APOSTLES

for Tom Murphy

We gathered in secret in Queens
one night at Professor Bill Frain's house
to meet with the outlaw priests
for anti-war prayer and strategy,
Frain's huge boxer
slobbering on the faithful
as we sat around the living room
discussing subversion and religion.
Dan's quiet power, Phil's powerful
disdain hypnotizing us.
We were the early
Christians come back to life.
Dan and Phil the new Apostles,
angry saints who would show us the way.

Dan, the holy one, took his rage
on the page, while Phil the fearless
found time for jail and marriage.
Once they were national news,
eluding the FBI, pouring blood
on government files, plotting
tirelessly in the name of Christ.
Kissinger hated them, Hoover
hunted them. We adored them.

They said you sometimes had to breach
good order to do the right thing.
Sometimes you had to break the law,
go to prison, to make your case.
They went on the run, went underground.

I was too scared to ever go to jail
for Jesus or the movement.
Even after belief lit up the room
and God came back to life that night
in Queens, in paranoid 1967.

DESIRE

He told me he was queer
and thought I knew. I was twenty-one.
He started to unbutton my shirt.
We were sitting on the couch in his apartment.
He said he would go off to places
where no one knew him
to have sex. Sometimes he'd
even dress in drag.

He was one of my heroes,
but no object of my desire.
Still, he argued and pleaded with me
to do this thing with him. So I took
my clothes off and got in his bed,
in dread of him.

I couldn't touch him,
the soft priestly flesh not what
I craved, and he was hurt
by my lack of interest.
I dressed quickly,
we smoked our Kents, he drove
me home. When he died,
tangled in his own brilliance,
I missed him instantly and wondered
if he'd ever found a way to find
himself in the lonely
house of the lord
where our sins wallpaper
the empty rooms.

Revolution

I sit in the back of the room smoking one cigarette
after another. It's Victorian lit, and there's a very sexy girl
in the class that I'm interested in. I wear an old army field jacket
and have a full beard. I scorn the system. It's 1968.
Even so, nearly everyone at Fordham but me seems straight.
In my whole time there, speeding toward a Ph.D. I never finish,
only one Jesuit taught me. Father Vincent Blehl, the world's
leading Cardinal Newman expert. I live in my first
apartment a few blocks from campus on Valentine Avenue.
I eat pizza every day for lunch under the El by Lamb's
bookstore, by the entrance to Rose Hill. All day
I read books, smoke, and study. Sometimes friends
come by and we get high. We want revolution.
We want to transform America. I volunteer for Gene McCarthy,
but mostly stay in my apartment and read. I go down to campus
a few times a week for classes. I'm not taking crap from
anyone, Jesuits included. When Father Blehl shows up for
his first class, he begins reading us what seem to be his old
grad school papers. He drones on and on for an hour
and a half. No one interrupts, questions him.
I smoke and fume. Then finally raise my hand.
He looks up, and the class comes to a halt. I can tell the sexy
coed is wondering what I'll say. Blehl is annoyed that I
have interrupted his monologue. "Father, I hope you don't
plan to just read to us. We can read on our own." Blehl
is visibly shaken and angry. If he could beat me with a stick
and get away with it, he would. I wonder what he is going to
do. Finally, glaring at me, half rising from his chair, he says,
"OK, Mister, put out that cigarette. No more smoking in here."

ORBIT

The girls of Daly Avenue were beautiful and tough.
They could kick your ass at twelve,
would make out with you at fourteen.
But they would not go all the way.
When I meet them now in the school auditorium
on Sunday afternoon at a benefit for the old parish
they are big, earthy, full of life. They test you
at every turn. They are smarter, wiser, funnier.
The men are haunted by the past,
the women rooted in the right now, right this minute.
There is nothing sadder than an old man
sneaking a smoke in the parking lot. There is nothing
sexier than an old girlfriend wrapping you in her arms
and whispering: you can take me now if you want, now.

CEREMONY

When I got married, we didn't know what to do.
We thought we needed a priest, but my wife isn't
crazy about priests, at least Catholic ones. Her father
tried too hard to shove Catholicism down the throats
of his kids, so they all veered towards the Methodism
of her mother. Not that my mother-in-law knows
what Methodism is all about. "Well, they have a method,"
she once told me. My wife liked all the singing the Methodists
did. She thought that was a very good sign.

So we compromised. We asked an Episcopalian priest
to marry us. To my wife, he was a Protestant, and that
was in his favor. To me, he was Episcopalian, which
meant he still had the power, could still do valid
sacraments in the eyes of the Catholic Church.
Since I hadn't been to Mass in 20 years,
I'm not sure why either of us needed religion
to be part of the picture. But we did.

So we visited Father William Wendt at his residence.
He was a famous man in Washington. He preached
the inevitability of death and sold bookcases that
conveniently converted into coffins when the time came,
which he assured us it would, a reality that I have spent
my whole life in terrified acceptance of.

At the ceremony itself, held in my brother's house
on a fair November day, I experienced the most
embarrassing moment of my life, but didn't know
it until after the fact. Unlike other men of the cloth,
Father Wendt did not say every three words for the bride
and groom, which each would then repeat. I wish he had.

Instead, he left it up to us to say the whole thing
from memory. I, apparently, announced with great
conviction that "I, Susan," would take "you, Terence,
to be my wife." When one of the guests cheerily
informed me, immediately after the deed was done,
of this most ridiculous bunglement,
which must have had the whole room repressing
its collective shock and amusement, I was
sick with self-deprecation. The most potent
moment of my life, and I screwed it up.

Father Wendt seemed to have a good time,
but as the post-ceremony turned into an Irish party,
with booze and Guinness galore, and a host
of friends banging out tunes in two or three rooms,
he informed me that he had to be taking off.
It was then that I added to my day's store of faux-pas.
"Whaddu I owe you, Father?" I asked, the Bronx
in me brimming forth. He was literally taken aback,
leaned a bit away from me, and announced,
in a tone the Pope might use to denounce contraception,
"We do not charge for the sacraments."

I stammered, realizing my terrible mistake.
"Of course, Father," I said. "I'm very sorry."
I took a drag on my cigarette. Think, you idiot, think,
I urged myself, as Father Wendt folded his shawl.
He reminded me a little of David Susskind.
"Father, may I make a donation to your church?"
"Certainly," he replied. "That would be appreciated."

Breath flowed back into my lungs.
I wrote the check, and he exited quickly out of the house,
the guests now mostly Catholic and sufficiently anesthetized
so that property damage and mayhem could commence.
Married, happy, co-star (for the day) of my universe,
I felt as blessed as a newly baptized newborn.

FAITH

In the linoleum there are alligators
when his mother comes to him at night.
Inside the apartment is a long hall
that turns halfway, the mother walking
the hall holding onto the walls
so she will not fall. In her bed
she grows old, swells up,
hair grows on her like a man.
In the early hours of a dark mid-
December day, she begins to fail.

Outside, on the street, stands the convent.
The nuns entrap the children, trick
them into going to the A&P, invite
them into the parlor of the convent.
A whiskered nun stands on the
convent steps waiting to catch children
to run errands. An old nun keeps
the convent clean. She washes floors
and dishes, polishes old wood. She is
the nuns' nun. The nuns cannot touch
each other, but they touch the children
when they can. There are small nuns,
fat nuns, nuns who play the piano,
queer nuns, singing and flying nuns,
old nuns, young nuns, dumb nuns,
fun nuns, attack nuns who smack and whack,
holy nuns who help the poor, sexy nuns
who know the score, departed nuns
we will see no more.

The best nuns of all are the Dominican
Sisters of the Sick Poor, who appear
every day at our door, each one a real
nurse, easing my mother's pain and fear
as she grows worse and worse
before she disappears and is seen no more
except in dreams, and even then
as a stranger on a distant shore
where we will sail to meet her
when the darkness is dispelled,
our souls opening like fists
our frail faith set free at last.

II. Nuns

MOTHER MARGARET MARY

        taught kinder-
garten and was said
to have a way with
five-year-olds

she had a thick beard

the stiff white head-
dress gave her beard
a blue tint

she would stand at the convent door
and wait for children to recruit
to run errands for the nuns

children got very good
at not seeing her
since once she caught
your eye
you were on your way
to the A & P

THE PRINCIPAL

whenever the principal entered
the room everyone had to stand up

the boys would bow
the girls would curtsy
and everyone had to say in unison

"good morning Reverend Mother
how are you Reverend Mother?"

MOTHER BERCHMANS

       was very sincere
so everyone made fun
of her
she taught
the sixth grade
and spoke in heavy "s" sounds
when things got
out of hand
Mother Berchmans
would say
admonishingly

"boyce and girlce—
be good!"

MOTHER AUGUSTINE

was my teacher
in the fourth grade
she was acerbic
and tough but had
a good sense of humor

at ten o'clock every
morning a student
would be appointed
to sell pretzels
to the class out
of a big cardboard
box
they were three
for a nickel

I broke the pretzels
up and nibbled on the pieces
for an hour or more

salt from the pretzels
would accumulate in my
shirt pocket and when
the pretzels were all gone
I would start eating
the salt out of my shirt

I have always loved salt

one day Mother Augustine
noticed me taking something
out of my shirt pocket
and putting it in my mouth

she stopped the class
"Mr. Winch, what are you eating?"
she said
I said, "nothing"

she insisted she saw me eating
something
I told her I wasn't eating anything

(I didn't really think of salt
as food, as something you "ate")

things got pretty intense
but finally she gave up
and dropped the whole matter

I think Mother Augustine
was a little fucked up
because she once grabbed
my ass and said something
which I now forget but
which then struck me
as kind of dirty

MOTHER NICHOLAS

was shocked

she noticed that some
of the boys were writing
things down while the man
was in the classroom
measuring us for caps and gowns

when the man left she snatched
a piece of paper from one of the boys
I think it was John Kelly
The paper had numbers written on it
She found other papers with numbers
written on them

She demanded to know what the numbers
referred to.
She said no one
would leave the classroom
until she found out

everyone was silent
time passed tension mounted

She started to become hysterical

finally one of the boys
spoke up
the numbers were the measurements
of certain girls in the class, he revealed

(just knowing the measurements
of Mary Ann Sherzan or Rose
Marie Russo was enough to make
any eighth grade boy drool)

Mother Nicholas was shocked
that the boys would do such
a thing   but she seemed
kind of excited herself
she gave us a heavy lecture
about sex

as it turned out
Johnny Wilson
with a forty-two
had the biggest bust
of all

III. O, Mary, I Could Weep for Mirth

PRAYER TO ST. PATRICK

St. Patrick, snake-hating Brit, forgive
us our sins, our wins, our losses,
forgive us our employees and bosses,
forgive us those stupid four-leaf clovers
that the ignorant confuse with the Holy Trinity-signifying
shamrock, especially around this time of year.
Forgive us green beer, Hostess cupcakes with green
icing, forgive us the moronic greening
of hair, food, water. Forgive us the total
lack of meaning that now attaches to your name.
It is all truly unseemly and insane.

Grant us a moratorium on any more news of
the triumphs of Michael Flatley or Frank McCourt.
God bless Paddy's pig and Paddy Moloney's wig,
Mickey and Andy Rooney, Rosemary and George Clooney.
Requiescat in pace, Versace et Liberace.
In nomine Dei, we've had enough of Leahy.
Dear saint of our isle, we'd like to send ya
an urgent plea to abolish Enya.

Let the bar owners pay
the poor musicians
a small fortune.
They're earning it.

Banish misfortune for the Irish
over here and the Irish over there.
While you're at it
banish "Danny Boy" and "The Unicorn."

Let there be an Irish-American fin de siècle
starring Mark McGwire and Margaret Heckler.
Grant another eighty-seven years to my Auntie Nora
and let history smile upon the Irish Diaspora.

Let the music be on the mark.
Lead the fiddle players from the dark
of orthodoxy. Oremus for my brother Seamus.
Let a thousand poems and songs
end the battles and undo the wrongs.

NUMBERS

1.
A math of holy numbers
ruled the cosmos.

Eternity could not be measured,
but our affronts to God could—
measured, weighed, totaled up,
matched with the right penance
and erased forever from our souls.

We were always confessing.
We would give them our numbers,
they would give us theirs:
5 our fathers, 5 hail marys,
a good act of contrition.

It all cancelled out for the moment,
until new sins started
accumulating—the supply of
fresh faults being limitless.

Say the Hail Holy Queen 10 times
and get 50 years plenary indulgence,
an advance parole from purgatory.
An incredibly good deal.
Devout people spent their lives
amassing indulgences.

The 7 proofs for the existence
of God, 7 deadly sins, 10 commandments,
12 apostles. We would kneel around
the bed and say the decades
of the rosary: 5 decades, 10 beads each.
The 9 First Fridays.

2.
It was a '50s thing—7 proofs, dwarfs,
types of ambiguity, deadly sins, brides for brothers,
samurai. It's rough not believing in the face
of all the proofs, the majestical roofs,
the unmoved moving.

God played by the numbers too.
One divine nature in 3 persons.
This mystery resisted understanding
except among the Irish, who found in
the shamrock the perfect metaphor for
the Trinity's challenge to the limits
of human mathematical ability.

SINNING

for Mick Moloney

When I was a young man I pursued every vice
from gluttony and envy to sloth
My behavior was certainly not very nice
but boys are all made of such broth
      Now that I'm older I've grown even worse
      than in the days of my humble beginnings
      I'll sing it & play it & recite it in verse
      that pleasure requires much sinning

I was raised a good Catholic in the reign of Pope Pius
and schooled under the thumbs of the nuns
who whacked us and smacked us till we cried out "God, why us?
we're just dutiful daughters and sons."
      But they'd look into our souls and see spiritual holes
      such voids that would set their heads spinning
      so they'd whack us some more till their hands became sore
      and we'd laugh 'cause we still loved our sinning

I recommend to you all if you like a good time
spent in serene contemplation
you try impure thoughts, an innocuous crime,
and top them off with fornication
      but there's all sorts of fun to be had on the run
      from childhood to the ninth inning:
      in addition to sex there must be, I would guess,
      a thousand more ways to be sinning

You don't see the trees resisting the breeze
you'll not catch the plants in denial
other creatures all do whatever they please
but humans would have them stand trial
      so be like the monkeys, the birds, and the bees

not to mention the fishes all swimming
take a page from creation's sweet pagan book
and devolve in an orbit of sinning

Wherever you go, put on a good show
and remember our time here is brief
if we'd all make enjoyment our main form of employment
it would offset the tears and the grief
so if you're down in the dumps, taking your lumps
always losing, never quite winning
take this message from me & set yourself free
with a dose of good healthy sinning

NIGHT SHIFT

My mother is working the graveyard shift as an elevator operator on 57th Street. She's fine for the first few hours, but around three o'clock in the morning she has all she can do to keep awake. So she goes down to the basement and washes her face in the sink and does some exercises. She does a few chin-ups and push-ups then goes back upstairs to the lobby. She reads a little, starts to fall asleep, drinks a cup of coffee from her thermos.

At four a.m. Mr. Jones from the ninth floor enters the lobby from the street. He is an antique collector. He is so drunk that he crawls the whole length of the lobby until he reaches my mother. She is awake. She takes him up to the ninth floor. When they get there, Mr. Jones wants my mother to come inside with him. He has something to show her, he says. My mother refuses. Mr. Jones then crawls into his apartment.

My mother wears a uniform. She wears bell bottom blue jeans, a fancy coat with brass buttons, high heel shoes. This is a requirement for elevator operators. All elevator operators must wear this same uniform. My father works as a porter at 550 Park Avenue. He too wears a uniform, though it is different from my mother's. His is gray. Both he and my mother try to keep awake.

At about four thirty a.m. the Monsignor arrives at the building where my mother works. He has the results of the tests they have run on my mother. My mother says, "What's the verdict?" The Monsignor says, "We'll see." The Monsignor says again, "We'll see."

Then my mother notices something strange about the Monsignor's face. His face is a large clock, with one hand much larger than the other. My mother stares intently at the Monsignor's face. She wonders if it's quitting time yet.

Never Able to Get Back

She's ironing, flicking water
on the wrinkled shirts my father
needs for Mass. The day
deposits huge deliveries of sun
into the front room. She glows
in a yellow painting of light.

We are on a tear. Splashing
each other, two boys in search
of a tunnel through the mind's eye
to the child's exchange of pure soul.
Energy injects us with its terrible
love of going and doing. She admonishes
us from that frozen photo in the past.

We do not see, we do not hear.
Blood turns our scalps red. We run
down the stoop into the future.
Coal is sliding down the chute
into the basement, turning the air
black. The light is a heavy
burden to my eyes. When I finally
blink, I behold mothers fainting
on the street. I see the boy
taken by the hand and led
into the dark parlor, where
he is dressed in white
that swaddles his body
in quiet repose
as silent as snow.

FAITH HEALING

Blackest day of the year. He must obey the rules today.
First: forget everything that has happened since 1962.
Second: go out and buy cigars and wine. Skip work.
Wait for the rain to stop. Don't make fun of religion.

Every night at exactly seven p.m., he calls the Virgin Islands.
This has been going on for as long as he can remember.
Before dialing, he practices all the necessary thoughts:
no fear, acceptance, no need for approval, exquisite manners.

He believes in God for 24 hours one day a year. This is that day.
He hears her voice telling him there is hope, love, eternal life.
He remembers the Host dissolving on his wet tongue,
so inside him it made his sick soul squirm.

Jesus

Jesus was everywhere
Whenever I said the name
        JESUS
I would bow my head
In all the pictures of Jesus
he always looks holy and boring
Jesus loved me, personally
This was apparently something
that was beyond his control
Jesus died in order to bring about
the salvation of mankind
Somehow, I guess because he was God,
the death of Jesus was considered
more important than other, ordinary deaths
Jesus was God, like I said, but actually
it was more complicated than that:
he was also the son of God
Jesus did not dance or sing
Whenever I would pass a church
I would make the sign of the cross

Jesus had a mother who was
referred to as the Blessed
Virgin Mary she was a simple
holy girl who was picked by God
to be the mother of his son
The Holy Ghost was also God
and appeared in most of his pictures
in the form of a bird
It was his job to bring about
the immaculate conception
and the virgin birth
two important concepts

that are very easy to get confused
Jesus was Jewish
Jesus never wore hats or smiled
A few times Jesus got very pissed off
Jesus never got married

Some people got more into Mary
than Jesus and why not
since Mary is the mediatrix
between human beings and God
Mary was assumed into Heaven
(the fastest way to get there)
In all the movies made in the nineteen
fifties about Jesus Mary always looks
pretty young though very holy
I don't remember anything that Mary
was supposed to have said
I don't even remember what language
Mary and Jesus spoke
I always think of Jesus
as speaking English I guess

HUMAN

We think of you in your place in the pietà,
full of sorrow, that grief unimaginable.
We think of you under glass, snake
at your feet, apple in the snake's mouth.
One bare sole of yours on the serpent's head.
We think of you ascending into Heaven
every time we see a rocket blasting off
from Cape Canaveral. We think of how
amazed (or upset or angry) you must
have been when a strange bird visited
you and it turned out to be the Holy Ghost
and somehow you were impregnated.
We hope no sex was involved. We think
of you in blue and white, God in your belly.
We think of you breaking the news
to Joseph, no man ever so cuckolded
as he. We think of other children you
must have borne, God's little half-brothers
and half-sisters. We think of you
eating bread dipped in olive oil,
a glass of wine on the side, listening
to music in the dark hills on a hot
night, laughing, a little drunk. We think
of you now, whole of body, sorrow
and tribulation behind you, wherever
Heaven might be, breathing in, breathing
out, wondering how a mere human
could wind up this way thousands
of years after God's grandma brought
you into the sad world of men.